BURM

OMETH*IN*G

MA

WENT

WRONG

BURMA

Preface *by Jeffrey Hoone*

Timing is a quality most often associated with the performing arts. The ability of an actor or musician to know precisely when, or for how long to hold a beat, prolong a look, or let silence fill the room, can mean the difference between a good performance and a great one.

Timing is virtually an invisible quality in the visual arts, but over the past few years Chan Chao's photographs have encouraged a wave of precise timing between individuals and organizations that have led to the production of this publication. From John Gossage, to the Open Society Institute, to Alice George, to Light Work, to JGS, Inc., and finally to Chris Pichler and the Nazraeli Press – Chao's photographs have helped us all find a way to collaborate in presenting this important body of work.

Chan Chao's family left Burma for the United States when he was 12 years old. Eighteen years later Chao returned to Burma with the intention of rediscovering and reconnecting with the culture and people he had left years before. Twice denied a visa by the Burmese government, Chao eventually made his way to the Thai-Burmese border where students had established several camps to launch guerrilla attacks against the military regime that controlled Burma with the goal of restoring democracy to the country.

With the knowledge that Burma's military junta is one of the world's worst human rights violators, Chao's portraits are remarkable for the sense of calm and tenderness that he draws out of each of his subjects. Each portrait is made from an intimate distance, generously placing each subject in the center of the frame surrounded by the soft focus of the lush jungle beyond. In many of his portraits the subjects hold simple objects: a sickle, a saw, a large piece of fruit, a live chicken. These simple objects provide an elegant solution to the problem of portraiture where individuals are often unsure of what to do with their hands, and in that uncertainty convey stiff and formal poses. But the objects are also disarming because they signal the activities of a simple agrarian life, not one of armed resistance. This contradiction plays heavily into the power that each image conveys, because each person that Chao photographs displays a remarkable range of honesty and emotion that seems to long for a return to the simple pleasures of family, work, and relaxation – not another night of firing rockets or setting land mines.

Given the political and military circumstances in Burma, Chao could have followed the lead of photographers like Susan Meiselas and Bill Burke whose gritty and dramatic images chronicling rebel resistance in Nicaragua and Cambodia have received wide praise and attention. But Chao's portraits have more in common with the simple style of August Sander's portraits of German workers and Fazal Sheikh's evocative images of refugees in Northern Kenya.

Chao's goal for this project is to bring greater attention and awareness to the democracy movement in Burma. It is hoped that the publication of the work here will help him realize that goal. Public awareness is only one ingredient necessary to resolve conflicts or end tyranny. Chan Chao has provided us with that essential ingredient and has challenged us to add to the mixture with force and resolve.

THE PHOTOGRAPHY OF CHAN CHAO

Kyaw Nge and Tun Aung, May 1997

Tin Taw Liang, January 1998

Thaung Tin and Friend, May 1997

Member of KNU, August 1996

Naing Soe, August 1996

Zaw Lin Htway, May 1997

Myo Win, May 1997

Biak Hlun, January 1998

Naing Win, May 1997

Tin Win, May 1997

Myint Oo, May 1997   *Saw Nay Htoo, June 1997*

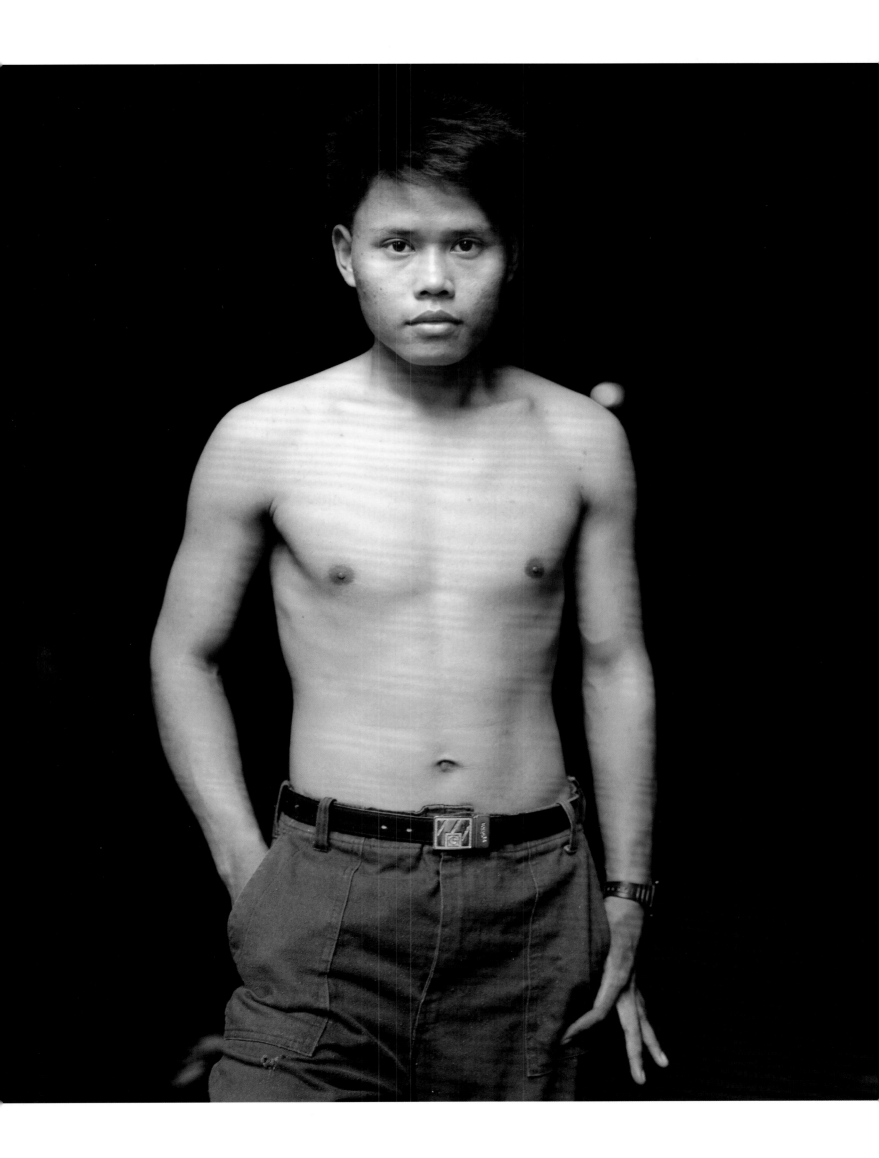

IN THE MOUNTAINS

Maung Lay, August 1996

Member of KNLA, August 1996

Hal Aye, August 1996

David, August 1996

Phaw Pha, May 1997

Tlim Na, January 1998

33

INTO THE JUNGLE

Saw Htoo "Abba", June 1997

Win Soe, May 1997

Member of ABSDF, May 1997

Member of KNLA, August 1996

Myo Than Htun "Super", May 1997

Mya Khaing, May 1997

41

Members of CNA, January 1998   Moe Thee Zun, August 1996

IN THE CLOUD

S

Aung Moe Zaw, August 1996

U Myint Zaw, August 1996

U Tin Aung, August 1996

Zaw Zaw, August 1996

Zaw Zaw Htun, May 1997

Member of CNA, January 1998

Member of ABSDF, May 1997

Member of KNLA, August 1996

Sein Win Tin and Nay Htoo, June 1997

Tun Aung Kyaw, August 1996

U Aye Saung and U Saw Jacob, August 1996

Hla Han, May 1997

Thant Zin Oo, May 1997

Ko Ye, August 1996

Aung Saw, May 1997

Thomas Thangno, January 1998

Thang Zen, January 1998

Karenni Girl, June 1997

Pado Mhan Sha, August 1996

Thein San, May 1997

Solomon, January 1998

UPON   THE

RIVER

Hla Toe, Wai Linn Zin and Thaung Htike, May 1997

U Myint Swe, June 1997

Thein Oo, May 1997

Young Buddhist Monk, June 1997

Nyi Nyi and George Abel, June 1997

Nyunt Nyunt and Hla Ya Min, May 1997

Than Than Win, May 1997

Naw One, May 1997

Kyaw Htoo and Robey, June 1997

Dr. Cynthia Moung, June 1997

Aung Ko and Yan Naing, May 1997

Sai Aung, Saw Hlaing and Aung Lwin, June 1997

Zaw Min Thu, June 1997

Young Recruit for CNF, January 1998

Young Recruit for CNF, January 1998

Soe Myint, December 1997

Aung Naing Oo, August 1996

Benjamin Turing, January 1998

Micho, January 1998

Thaung Han and Myat Soe, May 1997

Htun Htun Naing and Maung Nyo, May 1997

UNDER THE

THREAT OF ARMS

Ram Thang, January 1998

Ko Sonny, June 1997

Khawma, January 1998

Ni Lian, January 1998

SOMETHING WENT WRONG IN BURMA

Afterword *by Amitav Ghosh*

Like many Indians I grew up on stories of other countries: places my parents and relatives had lived in or visited before the birth of the Republic of India in 1947. To me the most intriguing of these stories were those that my family carried out of Burma. Several relatives, near and distant, had lived in that country before the Second World War. They'd fled to India in 1941 and 1942, just before the Japanese occupation. Even though many of them had suffered greatly, they always spoke of Burma as though it were a lost paradise: "Burma is a golden land, the richest country in Asia, the envy of its neighbors, its people are the kindest, most hospitable on earth . . . "

Yet none of my relatives ever went back, even for a visit. General Ne Win, the man who would become Burma's long-time dictator, had seized power in 1962. Almost immediately he'd slammed the shutters and switched off the lights: Burma had become the dark house of the neighborhood, huddled behind an impenetrable, overgrown fence. It remained shuttered for three decades.

Burma is one of the largest countries in Southeast Asia, with a land area considerably greater than that of Thailand, and a population of some forty-six million people. It hangs mango-shaped between India, China and Thailand, with the province of Tenasserim trailing like a tendril down the Malay peninsula. Its border with India is several hundred miles long. Yet, in defiance of the laws of proximity, General Ne Win was able to render his country just as invisible to its neighbors as it was to the world at large.

I first travelled to Burma in December 1995. By this time the country had been renamed Myanmar and its capital, once known as Rangoon, had become Yangon. The day after my arrival in Yangon I sought out a place that had figured large in my relatives' tales of that city: it was a small Hindu temple in the center of the city.

The temple was all but empty on the evening of my visit: a few elderly men were seated around a table in the echoing neon-lit hall. I introduced myself and mentioned some of my relatives' names. They gave me a warm welcome and invited me to join them at the table. They began to reminisce and the conversation soon turned to pre-war Burma. "Burma is a golden land," they said, using exactly the same words that I'd heard on the lips of my 'Burmese' relatives, "its people are the kindest, most hospitable on earth . . . "

How did it all go wrong? I asked. What happened? Historically Burma was a very rich country, with a superabundance of natural resources – oil, timber, minerals, gemstones. In the pre-colonial past, it had almost universal adult literacy and a rich literary culture. Now it was the most impoverished country in the world's fastest-developing region; one of the UN's ten least developed nations on earth, and a byword for repression, xenophobia and civil abuse. How could any country travel so far back so fast?

The man seated next to me was well over seventy, a thin, upright man with a thatch of white hair. He led me to the temple's entrance and pointed across the street, toward the dark, unlit compound of the Secretariat Building, a sprawling complex of decaying red-brick, administrative offices, built by the British at the turn of the century. "Do you see that balcony there?" he said, pointing at a second-floor corridor directly across the darkened street. "That was where Burma's future ended. Do you see that door? It leads to the room where General Aung San was assassinated on July 19, 1947. I was just down the corridor: I saw his body lying there."

General Aung San was the hero of Burma's independence movement. At the time of his death Aung San was thirty-two years old, a strikingly good looking young man, with high cheekbones, a receding hairline and a good-humored but determined glint in his eye. Despite his youth Aung San was then already the country's acknowledged leader: a few years before, as a young student-politician he had fled from British-ruled Burma and formed a tactical alliance with the Japanese. He was instrumental in organizing a small militia of Burmese students – hence the title 'General.' In 1942 he had marched across the border at the head of the Burma Independence Army with the invading Japanese forces. Later, becoming increasingly distrustful of the Japanese, he and his soldiers had switched loyalties and joined the Allies.

At the end of the war it was generally assumed that General Aung San would assume Burma's leadership after independence. He alone among his contemporaries possessed an appeal that extended beyond his own ethnic group, to the vastly diverse array of Burma's peoples. Aung San was by birth a Burman and thus a member of the country's largest single ethnic group. The Burmans are predominantly Buddhist and form two-thirds of the country's population. There are four sizable minorities – the Karen, the Rakhine, the Shan and the Mon – and many smaller groups, such as the Karenni and the Chin. Some are Buddhist, and are linked with the people of neighboring Thailand. Others, such as the Kachin, the Karen and the Karenni include Christians, mainly from families that were converted by American Baptist missionaries in the nineteenth century. And in the west there is also a substantial Muslim population.

What these vastly different groups have had in common, historically, is a fear of domination by the Burmans. Aung San uniquely was able to transcend the minorities' mistrust of Burman politicians: it probably helped that he happened to be married to a Christian, Daw Khin Kyi, although a devout Buddhist himself. In April 1947 Aung San led his recently formed political party, the Anti-Fascist People's Freedom League, to a resounding victory in the country's first general elections. He was thirty-two; he had been married nearly five years and had fathered three children. Three months later he was assassinated while attending a meeting of his cabinet-in-waiting. Six members of his cabinet died with him, among them some of the country's most respected politicians, including a few of its most important minority leaders. The assassins' identities were never discovered.

The Union of Burma attained its independence on schedule, in January 1948. U Nu, a trusted friend of Aung San's, took over the leadership of his party and was sworn in as Burma's first Prime Minister. Burma's civil war started three months later, with a massive Communist uprising. The ethnic insurgencies started in earnest a year later, in 1949, when a group of Karen rebels seized an armory on the outskirts of Rangoon and dug themselves in against government troops. Two Karen regiments of the Burma Army mutinied and they were soon joined by a regiment of Kachins.

In colonial times, British recruiting policies had favored minority groups over the majority population of ethnic Burmans. As a result, at the start of the civil war, the insurgents actually outnumbered government troops. The Karen and Kachin regiments also happened to be the elite units of the old Burma Army; they were led by some of its most talented officers and manned by seasoned veterans of the Allied campaigns against the Japanese.

In the initial stages of the conflict, the insurgents made short work of the U Nu government's inexperienced, understaffed army. They captured Mandalay, Burma's second city, within six weeks and then advanced on Rangoon, the capital, which was already under siege, caught between Communist insurgents and Karen rebels. A year after independence, the authority of the Burmese government extended no farther than the city's outskirts. The administration came to be nicknamed the Rangoon Six-Mile government. That it was able to survive at all was because of the timely arrival of an arms shipment from India.

General Aung San may well have been the only Burmese leader who could have averted the civil war. A few months before his death he had succeeded in negotiating a landmark treaty with representatives of several minority groups. He was able to persuade them that minority rights would be protected in a federal union. The resulting treaty, known as the Panglong Agreement, was ratified by several ethnic organizations, and it laid the groundwork for what could well have been a workable federal union. With General Aung San's assassination the Agreement collapsed.

Despite the strains of the civil war Burma held on to its federal, parliamentary constitution as it stumbled through the next fourteen years: elections were held regularly and the press flourished. Then, in 1962, General Ne Win, the chief of the army, abruptly took control of the government and suspended the constitution. Soon afterwards the new regime announced that its ideology was to be 'The Burmese Way to Socialism,' a bizarre mix of xenophobia, Marxism, ritual and astrology.

The people of Burma resisted military rule from the start. Within weeks of General Ne Win's coup of 1962, the students of Rangoon University sealed off their campus and declared it a 'fortress of democracy.' The police opened fire killing an unknown number of students. Large numbers of students fled to the border areas and joined forces with ethnic insurgents.

History repeated itself on a larger scale twenty-six years later. In March 1988, a brawl in a teashop provoked a clash between university students and riot police. The students responded by taking to the streets in protest against the regime: thus began Burma's democracy movement – as a spontaneous uprising against General Ne Win's decades' long dictatorship.

Soon after the start of the protests General Aung San's only daughter, Suu Kyi, arrived in Rangoon. Aung San Suu Kyi was two when her father died. Subsequently, much of her life had been lived abroad – in India, the United States, Britain and Japan. Through all those years she had returned regularly to Burma to visit her aging mother in Rangoon. It was news of her mother's hospitalization that brought her to Burma in 1988.

Pictures of General Aung San were a prominent feature of the student-led demonstrations for democracy. The assassinated nationalist had himself begun his political career as a student leader: the generation of students who formed the nucleus of the democracy movement of 1988 were quick to lay claim to his legacy of political activism and protest. Aung San Suu Kyi's family house quickly became a hive of political activity.

Demonstrations against the regime continued over several weeks, eventually forcing the resignation of General Ne Win. The scale of the protests escalated upon the dictator's departure: strike centers were organized throughout the country and people poured out of their homes to participate in a new wave of meetings and marches. Perhaps the most important day in the history of the democracy movement was August 8: to this day many Burmese refer to it as the 'Four Eights movement' because of the date – 8/8/88. In response to a call for a general strike, thousands of people from many different walks of life walked out of their homes to join the protest demonstrations. That night the army made its first concerted attempt to crush the movement by shooting down hundreds of unarmed demonstrators. The indiscriminate killings went on for four days, but demonstrators continued to flood the streets.

Aung San Suu Kyi formally announced her entry into the movement on August 26, in her speech at the Shwe Dagon Pagoda. "I could not, as my father's daughter, remain indifferent to all that was going on," she told the hundreds of thousands of people who had gathered to listen to her. "This national crisis could, in fact, be called the second struggle for independence."

On September 18 the army struck back: a group of senior military officers took control of the government and announced the formation of a 'State Law and Order Restoration Council.' The first move of the new junta – always referred to by its sinister acronym, SLORC – was to launch a carefully planned military operation against the democracy movement: army units took control of the streets by machine-gunning unarmed crowds and arresting hundreds of activists. A mass exodus resulted.

The formation of SLORC and the crackdown on the democracy movement came a bare three weeks later. In seizing power SLORC committed itself to holding elections in the near future. In response, Aung San Suu Kyi and her associates formed a political party, the National League for Democracy. Aung San Suu Kyi rapidly emerged as the party's single most important voice, repeatedly stressing the themes of human rights, democracy and non-violent activism.

Over the next several months Aung San Suu Kyi toured the country tirelessly, campaigning in anticipation of the promised elections. She drew vast crowds at every appearance and her popularity became a matter of increasing concern for the regime. On July 20, 1989, the day after the forty-second anniversary of her father's death, she was put under house arrest and barred from taking part in the elections. As it turned out, her disenfranchisement did not have the effect the junta had hoped for. When elections were eventually held, in 1990, her party won eighty per cent of the seats. With its ouster imminent, SLORC refused to countenance the verdict: in a flagrantly illegal move, the junta annulled the election results. Aung San Suu Kyi was offered safe passage out of the country on the condition that she never return.

In defiance of SLORC's efforts to force her into exile, Aung San Suu Kyi chose to remain in Rangoon: her house arrest continued for another five years. In that time she became a living symbol of Burma's predicament. In 1991, while still under detention, she was awarded the Nobel Peace Prize. Effectively, as of the time of writing, she is still under house arrest.

In the aftermath of the military crackdown, tens of thousands of students and activists fled to the remote and relatively inaccessible border regions of Myanmar. In these areas the civil war that had started after Burma's independence still raged unabated and large tracts of territory were under the effective control of ethnic insurgents. A Karen group had even founded a state, Kwathoolei,

on the southern reaches of the Salween river; to their immediate north, the Karenni controlled a sizeable chunk of territory. In the far north of the country, the borderlands were ruled by the Kachin; in the west, on the Indian border, it was the Chin who held sway. Many refugees from the democracy movement found shelter in these areas; many of them eventually chose to make common cause with the insurgents.

It is this grim, shadowy, large-unnoticed conflict that has shaped the faces of the people who figure in Chan Chao's remarkable portraits. Many of Chan Chao's pictures were taken in the area around the Thai border town of Mae Hong Son. I visited this area in 1996, at a time when SLORC had launched a vigorous military offensive against the group that had held this part of the border for most of the last fifty years – the Karenni National Progressive Party (KNPP). Allied with the KNPP was a small 'regiment' of student refugees, manned by former activists from the democracy movement. It was this group that had offered to take me across the Myanmar border, into one of the Karenni-held areas that was currently under attack.

The Burmese offensive was in its second week when I flew to the border town of Mae Hong Son, in northwestern Thailand. It was a clear day and I watched in awe as the red, riverine plains of the south changed into jagged, densely-forested mountains, a pristine landscape of misted valleys and towering ridges. I could see no sign of habitation until Mae Hong Son appeared suddenly in my window, a string of teakwood buildings nestled in a deep valley, like a runnel of sand in a cupped palm.

In Mae Hong Son, I was met by a guide, a member of the student-regiment. He had been briefed to lead me to the commander of his unit, who was in a forward camp near the Karenni front line. We rented a motor-scooter and went rattling off down a dirt track that ended at a small village at the foot of the mountains. We waded across a stream and started climbing. It was about five in the afternoon and the sun had already dipped behind a ridge. Soon, following a steeply ascending mountain trail, we stepped from twilight into the darkness of a densely canopied forest. By the time we finally stumbled into the students' base camp, hours later, fatigue had erased all thought from my mind. It was all I could do to stay on my feet.

Half-a-dozen young guerrillas were squatting around a campfire, by a bamboo hut, dressed in camouflage fatigues and playing guitars. A heavy-set, thickly bearded man detached himself from the group and stepped up to meet me, holding out his hand. He introduced himself as Ko Sonny, the commander of the regiment.

He looked me over as I sat panting on a rock. After a moment's hesitation he asked, a little shyly: "Are you Indian?" It was then that I noticed that his spoken English sounded oddly like my own.

I nodded, and through a veil of exhaustion, took another look at him. Suddenly I sat up. "And you?" I said, in mounting surprise.

"My parents were Indian," he said, with a smile. "But I'm Burmese."

His given name, I learned, was Mahinder Singh; Sonny was a family nickname which he'd adopted because it was easier to pronounce. He was in his early thirties and had been 'in the jungle' almost eight years. His family had been settled in Burma for three generations. His parents were both born there; his father was Sikh and his mother Hindu, both from families of well-to-do Indian businessmen.

I felt oddly disconcerted listening to Sonny's story in the flickering firelight. I was sure our relatives had known each other once, in Burma: his had opted to stay and mine hadn't. But for a few years and a couple of turns of fate we could have been in each other's place.

I spent the night on a spare bamboo palette in Sonny's hut. The next day I was jolted awake a little before dawn by the sound of a Burmese artillery barrage. Groping for a match, I stepped outside to find Sonny talking urgently into a walkie-talkie. He told me the Burmese army had launched an assault on a Karenni position in an adjoining valley. The fighting was a good distance away, but the sound of gunfire came rolling up the misted mountainside with uncanny clarity, the rattle of small-arms fire clearly audible in the lulls between exploding artillery shells. The noise sent flocks of alarmed parrots shooting out of the mountainside's tangled canopy. With daybreak I had my first look at the camp – a string of thatched bamboo huts arranged village-like along a mountain stream. It was evident that a great deal of thought had gone into the camp's planning. The plumbing for example, was far from rudimentary, with water being piped directly into bathrooms and showers from a nearby stream. Downstream lay a dammed pond, teeming with fish, and a pen full of pigs. Next to each hut was a vegetable patch, with a neat little label on a stick. Once Sonny had ascertained that the fighting was not headed our way, he picked up a tin watering can and waded into a patch of sprouting bok choy. Following his lead the others put aside their battle gear and disappeared into their pumpkin trellises and mustard beds, like a troop of Sunday gardeners, armed with trowels and watering cans.

"Growing food," Ko Sonny explained, "is just as important to our survival as fighting. We have to do this before we go on patrol."

We set out an hour or so later, with a detachment of half a dozen student fighters. Sonny was in the lead, dressed in fatigues and chewing on a cheroot. Once we had crossed the border, an unmarked forest trail, Sonny and his men reclaimed a cache of aging M-16s and slung them over their shoulders.

We climbed up to an overlooking ridge and I found myself gazing dumbstruck at a majestic spectacle of forested gorges, mountain peaks and a sky of crisp, pellucid blue. The shelling was sporadic now: occasionally the forest canopy would silently sprout a mushroom cloud of smoke, the accompanying blast climbing leisurely up the slope moments later. Mae Hong Son was clearly visible, through a delicate tracery of overlapping spurs and ridges, a smudge in the floor of a tip-tilted valley. Sonny pointed to the Karenni post we were to visit. It was called Naung Lon and it was built around a peak that reared high above the surrounding spurs and ridges. I wouldn't have recognized it as a guerrilla outpost: it looked more like a stockade designed to keep out elephants.

We entered through a gate hidden in a wall of sharpened bamboo stakes. After crossing a moat and a barbed-wire barrier we made our way gingerly to a ring of heavily sandbagged gun emplacements. We were met by a Karenni officer, a tall stooped man, with melancholy eyes and an air of regretful doggedness. He showed me around the camp, pointing proudly to a volleyball court and a sunken hall that served as both mess and chapel. The fighters' living quarters were in a warren of trenches, dug deep into the mountain's flattened tip.

The captain and his men – some of whom figure in Chan Chao's photographs – were all devout Christians. The captain himself happened to be a Baptist, his ancestors having been converted by American missionaries in the late nineteenth century, but there were also several Catholics among his men.

The captain's eyes flickered constantly over the thickly forested mountains around us as we spoke. His arm described a semi-circle as he pointed to the Burmese positions on the mountaintops around us. The Burmese had concentrated ten thousand men in the area, he explained, against this the Karenni army could muster a force of about six hundred. He clearly knew that he was defending a hopeless position; he had already made plans for its evacuation.

Later I remarked to Sonny that I could not see how the Karenni army could possibly escape defeat. To my surprise Sonny laughed. He'd grown up with the Karenni: he knew the insurgents well, their strengths and their weaknesses. The Karenni had been fighting against dire odds for fifty years, Sonny pointed out; since long before there was a SLORC. They had been fighting since World War II; many of them regarded the war against SLORC as a direct continuation of their earlier war against the Japanese. Some Karenni families had been at war for three generations and many of their fighters had spent their entire lives in refugee camps.

It was the second world war that thrust the Karenni suddenly center-stage on the continental theater. Looking for Asian partners in the struggle against the Japanese, the Allied powers armed several ethnic groups along the borders of Burma, encouraging them to rise against the occupying army. The Karenni, Karen and Kachin, all of whom had substantial Christian minorities, eagerly embraced the Allies. A number of British and American military personnel took up residence in their villages, deep in the mountains and forests, some of them virtually assuming the role of tribal elders.

The Karenni, along with the Karens and Kachin, were spectacularly effective fighters and their loyalty proved to be of major strategic importance to the Allies. The repayment these groups expected was independence and to this day they nurture a profound and bitter sense of historical grievance that the perceived debt was never repaid.

Many of the Karenni leaders I spoke to saw their struggle as a part of the unfinished business of World War II. One of their spokesmen, Mr. Abel Tweed, talked to me at length about the war. His voice shook as he talked of the British departure from Burma. "British people very cunning, very clever," he said, "they come, they sit, they eat and they kick you away."

The Karenni's sense of historic betrayal has been constantly reinforced by Burmese attempts at 'pacification' and by the rule of terror imposed on their state by the army. Over the years, in association with human rights organizations, the Karenni have kept a careful reckoning of the military regime's abuse of the civilian population: a ghastly litany of torture, surveillance, summary execution and forced labor. To varying degrees these conditions exist everywhere in Burma, among the Burman majority as well as the minority groups. But experts agreed that human rights abuses are at their most severe along the country's borders.

At the time of my visit, the six thousand strong Karenni population in Thailand was divided between five refugee camps run by the KNPP. Until a few years before, these camps were on the other side of border, in a narrow tract of land controlled by Karenni insurgents. The steady advance of Burmese troops had gradually pushed the encampments over the border, into Thailand.

Although the insurgents' manpower was drawn largely from these camps, Karenni fighters only took up arms once they had crossed back into Burma: they never carried arms or wore uniforms on the Thai side of the border. The camps were thus entirely civilian settlements, with large numbers of women and children. Their appearance was of tranquil, if impoverished mountain villages.

The Karenni camps were all clustered around Mae Hong Son – a town that had recently emerged as an important tourist center, with a special emphasis on an activity known as 'hill tribe trekking.' The Karenni refugee camps had come to be linked to this industry through a bizarre symbiosis. The women of one particular Karenni sub-group have traditionally worn heavy brass rings to elongate their necks. These women had become ticketed tourist attractions, billed as 'giraffe women.' The

refugee camps in which they lived were featured on all the local 'hill-tribe trekking' routes. In effect tourism had transformed these camps, with their tragic histories of oppression, displacement and misery, into counterfeits of timeless rural simplicity: waxwork versions of the very past their inhabitants had irretrievably lost. Karenni fighters, returning from their battles on the front-lines, became, as it were, mirrors in which their visitors could discover an imagined Asian innocence.

The Karenni refugees' principal source of income, until recently, was timber, from the border areas that were under its control. They granted logging concessions to Thai businessmen in exchange for a small fraction of the profits. It was these profits, senior Karenni officials explained, that lay behind the current escalation in the conflict. Burmese army commanders had recently negotiated their own deals with Thai timber companies: hence their determination to seize control of the insurgent's territory. In other words the war had resulted in a situation where the forest would be the loser no matter who won: either way, the jungles of the border are clearly headed for ecological ruin.

* * *

As a leader of a guerilla regiment, Sonny fit none of the stereotypes that came to mind. He was very good company, always witty, ready to laugh, enormously intelligent, and so completely devoid of militarist or macho posturing that it was easy to forget that he was in fact a hardened combatant, who had lived through eight years of jungle warfare.

Sonny's father was a government engineer, who'd spent much of his life in a tiny provincial town, Loikaw, the capital of Burma's erstwhile Karenni State. His mother was an active social worker who took a keen interest in politics: by Sonny's own account she was the formative influence in his life. Sonny's political involvement began in Rangoon, where he studied physics for five years. He had chosen to champion the cause of Karenni and other minority students in Rangoon. On returning to Loikaw after his Master's degree, he was instrumental in organizing peaceful pro-democracy demonstrations there in 1988. He was arrested on September 18, 1988, and released ten days later. Fearing re-arrest, he immediately started to plan his escape to the border. On the night of October 6, Sonny walked out of Loikaw with a small group of fellow democracy activists. The night he left, his mother told him that she would rather have him fight military rule than spend his life in jail. He never saw her again.

Led by a couple of Karenni students Sonny and his friends made their way to a rebel base. The insurgents gave them a warm welcome and provided them with land and supplies to set up bases of their own. Before leaving Loikaw neither Sonny nor his fellow-activists had ever so much as held a gun. But on reaching the border they formed an organization and decided to launch an 'armed struggle' against SLORC. In the beginning the student army numbered in the thousands, but it came to be severely depleted over time. Sonny and his sixty-man 'regiment' were among the last of its remnants. When I met him, Sonny had been fighting for eight years, during which he and his unit had been driven steadily back until they barely had a toehold on the border.

Sonny had no illusions about the military effectiveness of the 'armed struggle.' "We're fighting because there is no other way to get SLORC to talk," he told me. "For us armed struggle is just a strategy. We are not militants here: we can see how bad war is."

I asked, "Have you ever thought of trying other political strategies?"

"Of course I would like to try other things," he said. "Look: do you think I like to get up in the morning and think of killing? Killing someone who isn't working for himself, who is from my own country, who is forced to fight by dictators? Who loses when people from one country fight each other? The country. No human being wants to die. People want to survive. I would like to try other things – politics, lobbying. But the students chose me to command this regiment. I can't just leave them and go."

Over the last eight years Sonny had paid a severe personal price for his decision to leave Loikaw. His long-time girlfriend, in Yangon, had given up waiting for him and married someone else. By his own account the person he was closest to was his mother. She had helped sustain him through his time in the jungle by sending the occasional letter and the odd package of Indian food – mango pickle and wheat flour – to him with travelling merchants. Then, in 1994, his mother died of a sudden heart attack; Sonny found out months afterward from a passing trader.

"When I decided to leave," Sonny said, "I knew I would lose my life. But I had hope. When I first came to the jungle I thought it would be not more than five years before I saw my family again. My mother was just fifty-eight, quite strong and healthy. I never expected to hear that she would die."

I heard many similar stories amongst Sonny's fellow student-dissidents: stories of heartbreak, disappointment and increasing despair. In many ways the students' plight was worse still than that of the Karenni refugees, being devoid even of such consolations as family, marriage, and a functioning everyday life. When they were not on the front, the students were at their 'office' in Mae Hong

Son, where they lived four or five to a room. Yet they worked with tireless dedication, sending out an endless stream of letters, faxes, and e-mail, to keep the world informed of developments in their country.

Most of them were in their mid to late thirties. They had once aspired to careers as technicians and engineers, doctors and pharmacists. Those hopes were gone. They had no income to speak of, individually or collectively, and had to depend on international relief agencies for handouts of rice and fish paste. Their contacts with Thai society were few and invariably grim. They were decent, idealistic young men and women, who had once had fairly commonplace aspirations. Through a ghastly trick of fate they found themselves paying the price for the crimes of their country's self-appointed rulers.

I was not an unsceptical or partisan observer. I had little sympathy with the means that the insurgents had chosen: indeed it was evident to me that their 'armed struggle' would only serve to marginalise them in the future. I had many arguments on this score with Sonny and his comrades. Their struggle was harming them much more than SLORC, I told them; they would do well to rethink their options, for themselves and their movement. It took me a while to understand that this was a cruelly superfluous piece of advice. The truth was that they had very few options. Legally they were not allowed to either work or study in Thailand; to seek asylum abroad as refugees, they were required to enter a UN holding camp in southern Thailand while their papers were processed. Those whose applications were rejected ran the risk of being deported to Burma, where they were almost certain to be imprisoned, or worse. Their only remaining alternative was of joining the underworld of illegal foreign workers in Thailand, of vanishing into a nightmarish half-life of crime, drugs and prostitution. They had been pushed into a situation where the jungle seemed to be the sanest available alternative.

Chan Chao's portraits are remarkable for the honesty with which they portray the plight of the people who are trapped in this terrible conflict. In his pictures one sees despair, defeat, suffering and incomprehension; one sees also the courage, fatalism and hope that has sustained this war for more than half a century. As a record of human suffering, Chan Chao's portraits are as valuable as Roger Fenton's pictures of the Crimean war, Robert Capa's photographs of World War II and Sunil Janah's images of the Bengal famine of 1942.

I would like to thank the following people for making this book possible: A special thanks goes to John Gossage for his guidance, encouragement, and support throughout the project; Terri Weifenbach for her thoughtful reassurance; Jeff Hoone and Howard Stein who understood the need for this project to be seen, and responding to it; my Father for introducing me to the people in this book; Amitav Ghosh for his insightful essay; Chris Pichler for putting all of this together. And Jenny Cohan for her love and support. I also thank James Huckenpahler, Derry deBorja, Santay Saralak, Vumson, Bo Hla-Tint, Mary Panzer, Alice Rose George, Gary Hesse, and Mary Lee Hodgens. The Burma Project of the Open Society Institute and the Photography Department at The Corcoran School of Art, Carl Bower, Manuel Toscano, and Ken Ashton are to be thanked for their friendship.

— *Chan Chao*

Burma: Something Went Wrong is published by Nazraeli Press in association with Light Work. Book design by John Gossage and Chan Chao for The co.of. Photographs copyright 2000 by Chan Chao. Texts copyright the Authors. This edition copyright © 2000 by Nazraeli Press/Chris Pichler. Printed in China by O.G.P. for Nazraeli Press, 1955 West Grant Road, Suite 230, Tucson, Arizona 85745, USA. ISBN 3-923922-87-6